PREFACE

I once watched a cat catch a mouse that had almost gotten away. The mouse had run just in time into a hole at the bottom of an old grain bin. But then it had stopped, leaving about an inch of its tail sticking out behind. The cat was on that bit of tail like a flash, and dragged the mouse from the hole, its four feet scratching vainly along the floor.

This story, like the mouse, almost got away. In the summer of 1955 I was a young man of twenty, working in a little quarry on the Tug Hill Plateau of New York State, a tangle of hills, dense forest, and mostly abandoned hardscrabble farms about thirty miles east of Lake Ontario. My two friends and I lived in a white canvas wall tent next to the quarry — just a series of quartzite ledges, really, exposed by the small stream flowing past them.

We bought our milk, eggs, butter, and smoked ham from the woman who owned the land. She was seventy-two years old then, and had lived there since arriving as a bride at the age of fifteen.

She lived with her second husband in the farmhouse. As we got to know her better during the summer, she told us the story of his life. She was the only one who could have told it. Even then there were gaps in it, and like the mouse's tail, there was only a little sticking out. I grabbed it. A good thing I did, too. A couple of years later she was gone.

I have tried to fill in the gaps as best I could.

JUNE 1955 • OSCEOLA, NEW YORK

Back in the woods the black flies are fierce and clinging, whining in our ears and eyes. But out here in the quarry where we cut and load the stone, they leave us alone during the heat of the day. I push the kill button of the little gasoline air compressor, and the sound of its exhaust dies away. Silence returns to the clearing. I can hear the distant cries of crows, the throb of a tractor, and the bubble of the brook at the foot of the quarry.

I straighten up, bend over backwards to stretch, and descend stiffly to the brook, where I've left an empty pork-and-beans can hanging upside down on the stub of a broken branch beside a little waterfall. The water is sweet and icy, smelling of wet, green moss. I can feel it inside me, sliding down between my lungs into my stomach.

I replace the can on the twig. A last clear drop hangs off its rim, trembling. I touch my finger to it, and then to the tip of my tongue. I take off the blue bandana around my forehead and rinse it in the little basin at the foot of the fall. I use it to wash my face, and rinse it again.

Back up on the rock ledge, I wring out the bandana and drape it over the handle of a shovel to dry in the sun. Then I sit beside it to enjoy the silence and the view. The truck should be here soon to pick up the pyramid of cut stone beside me.

Far below me, the hill and the brook drop down to a pasture and stone walls being overwhelmed by the reclaiming forest. The course of the brook across the pasture is marked by a tangle of alder trees. Beyond it, a scruffy, unpainted farmhouse and barn and a glimpse of the road to Florence. And then lump after lump of jumbled hills, one behind another, crowding up against the west branch of Fish Creek on its turbulent way down through beds of ancient sandstone and shale to Oneida Lake off to the south.

The sky is blue — or must be, with the sun so bright. It's the kind of day that you don't look up; enough to feel the molten brass upon your back and shoulders. I drape the still-damp bandana over my head to shade my eyes and gaze down at the quiet farm below.

Hardly anything moves. A few cows stand in the shade of a dying elm, tails flicking at flies. Chickens dust themselves in the yard beside the shed, and a cat sits on the gray porch railing. I see it as if through glycerin, slow and silent as a dream.

The screen door opens, a man steps out, the door swings shut. He has taken two steps before the slap of the door carries up the hill to my ears. He shades his eyes with his hand, looking up in my direction, and starts to walk across the field. Here he comes.

A DREAM OF
DRAGONS

NORWAY, 1894

Olav — son of Erik Bjørnsson — seventeen,
swung his father's scythe and dreamed:

The singing scythe Grandfather Bjørn had made
and honed each time he found a bit of shade
and passed on to his oldest son
to pass on to his oldest son
to pass until there were no longer sons —
the scythe hissed like the grains of sand on the beach
that hiss when a wave falls back and the bubbles burst.

The wind that whispered through the grain
and dried the sweat upon his arms and chest
bore from the west the scent of salt
and the distant rumble of the Norwegian Sea.

The sound of the surf was often full of voices —
men's voices, shouting — speaking in words
that he could almost hear, an ancient tongue
that he could all but understand.
Now and then he heard them laugh and curse,
when an oar to windward catching the top of a wave,
the salt spray lashed across their faces
and ran glistening down their ruddy beards.

A lonely, quiet boy, his spirit stirred
by music no one else on the farm could hear.
Evenings found him standing on the cliffs,
still listening, while the sea breeze stirred his hair.
The sky dimmed to its long summer twilight,
and seemed to shimmer, as if a breeze
disturbed translucent curtains at a window.
A moment later the curtains caught fire,
and the lights were dancing in the sky!

It was almost time for him to go;
he could feel his heart beat in his ears.
A young dragon perched on the edge of its nest,
drying its wings in the wind from the sea.

But when he told his father how it was with him,
Gruff Bjørnsson laughed and bent to his work again.

Olav could see how it all would end:
It had been like this in Norway for a thousand years:
The tiny fjordside farms went to the oldest sons,
and the others found what livelihood they could.
The most adventurous younger sons built ships,
swift-sailing ships — some for trading, some for war —
and in the springtime rowed out through the breakers.
They filled their sails and slowly became tiny dots
upon the sea, and then were gone, sometimes forever.
A few of them returned, but most did not.
Their bones lay in the sea, or buried far away,
from Greenland to Constantinople.
Did it matter where? The Norns decree that cattle die, that
   all men die, and nothing lives on after them but fame.

The family sat at supper on an evening after milking.
Olav, the youngest, tall for his age, and strong,
but smarting and sullen from the never-ending work
that went around and round and never anywhere;
seeing too well what it did to men and women:
his father, crabbed and old before his time;
his mother, with nothing before her, wistful;
his brothers, jostling and jealous to be first,
cuffing him whenever they came close at work.
They'd given him a saga-name — Olav the Dreamer —
but had no inkling what it was he dreamed.

A beggar stopped at the gate, an old man with a cane —
they saw him through the open door —
dressed in rags, with a dirty bandage over one eye.
But before he could even lift his hand to speak,
Erik Bjørnsson rose and pointed down the road.
The old man turned wearily away, his good eye
taking them in — the angry father, the sad-faced wife,
the brothers watching silently. The watery blue eye
lingered a moment on Olav, who knew the insult
for the sacrilege it was. He left the house,
walked slowly down to the cliffs above the sea.
He listened to the nesting sea birds' screams
and the chafing of the surf on the rocks below.
He remembered afterward, but never said,
that this was the moment he knew he had to go.

Two summers he went with the fishermen,
far north along the coast, to the latitudes
where the sun at midnight off the Lofotens
never goes down, but only skims
the surface of the oily, heaving waves,
and then lifts off to go around again.
He learned to steer a compass course,
to ease the boat into a heavy sea,
to read the charts, such as they had aboard.

And always he was asking, what is that? —
how can you find the edge of deep water
just by the difference in the breaking seas?
Which way is Iceland? and the Faeroes? Point!
How do you follow the underwater ridge,
the Viking route that runs beneath the sea
and points the way to the land beneath the ice?
and — tell me! — is it true that you can smell
the smoking mountains many miles at sea?

Two winters he worked with Old Ulf Thorsson,
the boat-builder who lived beneath the hill
and puffed his pipe and closed his eyes
and rattled on about the many ships he'd built.

He showed Olav the holes in the rocks
where the dragon ships had moored in the fjord,
a thousand years before, waiting for spring;
the head of a battle-axe, huge and rusted black,
he'd found among the rocks along the beach.

Old Ulf, son of Thor, was an old-believer,
and knew all the sagas almost by heart —
of Grim and Gunnbjørn, and Erik and Leif,

who sailed west in their beautiful dragon ships
for a thousand kilometers, and then beyond,
a thousand years ago, in search of Thule.
Nobody ever could say what Thule meant;
it was a place just beyond the farthest land
that anyone had ever visited.
When Olav heard Old Ulf's voice begin to lift
in the cadence of the ancient skaldic rhyme,
he would stop to listen, entranced. That night
would find him on the cliff top, looking west.

Too tired to work for wages anymore,
Old Ulf was building himself a boat —
ten meters long, stout, and double-ended,
straked in curving pine like a dragon-ship,
she would rise to the waves like a resting gull —
the boat he'd waited all his life to build,
till now it was too late for him to use it.
That on a day that now would never come
would have filled her sails as she cleared the fjord,
lifted her bow to the North Atlantic swells,
and followed westward the wakes of the dragon ships
to the Shetlands, the Faeroes, Iceland, Greenland,
    Markland.

The names rolled well-rehearsed from Old Ulf's tongue,
each one a dream a little more impossible.
By the time his tongue spoke Vinland in the offing,
his heart knew he could never go himself.

And then one day in March, at the equinox,
sun streaming through the open door of the shop,
and the smell of shavings and varnish in the air —
they had finished the mast and boom and gaff —
Ulf and Olav were bolting iron hardware
to the deck and cabin house, Old Ulf outside
to drive the bolts through and set them in putty,
Olav inside to turn the nuts down tight.

They stopped for tea, sat side by side on the bench
in the sun in front of the shop, facing the fjord.
The tide was at the ebb. Two Arctic loons,
on their way north to their summer nesting grounds,
were fishing several meters off the dock.
Old Ulf and Olav watched quietly,
holding their mugs of tea between their hands.

"Will you be going north again to fish?"
Olav felt a tightness in Old Ulf's voice.

"Well, yes," said Olav, "I told them that I'd go."
His own voice seemed to belong to someone else.

Old Ulf was silent again. He lit his pipe.
"What if I were to give you this little boat?
Which way would you go then, my friend?"

It was not a question to be answered in a rush,
even though his heart was pounding in his chest.
So he waited and watched the pair of Arctic loons
until his voice at last came back to him.

"Over a thousand years ago, the men
with names like ours built boats right here,
and in the spring they left and sailed west
and watched their lovely homeland disappear,
till the highest mountain sank into the sea.

"They looked for land; they looked for liberty;
they looked for Thule. Some of them came back.
But many hundreds more did not come back.
With this boat I would look for the place they must
    have found.
And then I would sail beyond the farthest sagas."

Ulf puffed his pipe and raised his face to the sun.
His eyes were wet. "The boat is yours," he said.
"We need to find the money for the sails.
And soon. You need to be off by the first of May."

At noon that day he took a piece of rope
and held it up against the southern sky.
He tied one knot in it at the horizon,
another to cover the center of the sun.
"Now hold this up each day at noon," he said.
"If the sun is above it, you've turned south,
and if below, you're north of this latitude.
Each time you make a landfall, check the knots,
and set them again for where you want to go.

"Straight west one day and night if the wind is good,
beyond the deep Norwegian Trench offshore,
beyond the Viking Bank, where the sea heaves high,
are the Shetlands, islands where our people lived
a thousand years ago. Do not sail close.
Keep well off shore, for the seas may be foul.
The island of Unst is three hundred meters high
at its northern end. You'll spot it from far at sea.
It will make you lonely to see it and pass it by.

"But steer west by north for two more days and nights
and you'll be in the Faeroes, the islands of the sheep.
Make for the south side of the biggest one,
and stop there in the harbor to get fresh water.
The fishermen there are Danes, but speak Icelandic.
Thorshavn, it is called — the harbor of Thor,
and Ulf Thorsson would be there, but he cannot.

"Then west a little north for three more days,
and the smoking mountain, Hekla, will rise from the sea.
When the wind is right, you will smell the sulfur.
Another day, around the western cape,
and you reach the harbor of Reykjavik.

"But you cannot stay; you'll be almost out of time,
and the sea ahead of you is cold and dark.
Sail toward the west again, about a week.
Tie again the knot you used to get to Thorshavn;
the sun is lower now, but it will take you
to the southern tip of Greenland, Cape Farewell.
Head west when the knot is below the sun.
Dip your gaff in salute as you pass the cape,
for the bones of your fathers are buried there,
at Brattahlid, where they lived four hundred years,
the abandoned, forgotten orphans of Erik the Red.

"Beyond the cape you must be vigilant!
It is what they call the Sea of Labrador.
A current flows there like the one we have here.
Our current brings us warm water from the south,
helps us grow our hay and keeps the fjords from freezing.
The current there comes from the north. It is cold,
and brings with it great floating mountains of ice
that seem to move as if they had engines in them.
Sometimes they overturn. You must keep away!
You will be sailing in darkness again at night,
and you will be alone. You must not sleep while it is dark.

"But one more week of sailing west by south
through the icebergs coming down like great ships,
and you will raise the coast of Labrador —
grim, rocky land, with dark spruce down to tidewater.
Leif Eriksson in his farfaring ship coasted it south.
He called it Markland, the Forest Land;
beyond that Vinland, where our people settled once,
far from home, and found their spears and axes
no match for the arrows and anger of the natives there.
So they loaded their ships again and sailed away.
When you have arrived there, you are beyond my mind.
You have sailed to the end of all the sagas,
and from that place westward you must write your own.

"There is nothing more that I can tell or give you.
You have my boat, my compass, and all I know,
and the youth I should have used when it was mine.
Beneath the foot of the mast is a hammer of Thor,
and in every line of the hull a young man's dream."

Olav sold his share of the farm for sails.
The night before he left his mother's home
the lights were in the north again,
shifting, flaming, calling in the sky.
He knew where the dragon-men had gone,
and the bursting of his heart knew why.
He washed out to sea with the morning tide.

Alone with his boat and old Ulf Thorsson's compass,
with the highest mountain behind between his shoulder
    blades
and one unmoving star above him all night long.
A homesick boy cried for his mother's home.
But when one day at last he came to land,
the boy was gone, and the Iceland fishermen saw
a smiling, straw-haired, red-faced dragon man.

West of Iceland the sea turned cold,
but in just five days he saw the Greenland ice cap
rising above the heaving waves. Off Cape Farewell

the seas were higher than his stubby mast.
He wondered how those old Icelandic farmers
could have done it, in their open ships,
and then remembered: over half of them —
men, wives, children, livestock — were never seen again.

The Labrador Sea was strangely still, but stirred,
like a sleeping bear that could wake at any moment.
He held his course a little south of west,
astonished at the great, blue mountains of ice,
big as the Nidaros Cathedral in Trondheim,
that sailed ominously south without a wind
to drive them. He napped when he could
and spent the nights on watch, fighting sleep,
peering into the dark for looming shapes,
oars at the ready in case the breeze should fail him.
On the fourth evening he raised the Torngats,
impossibly black, and steeper even than the Lofotens.
He saw no settlements. The sea was beginning to freeze.

He set up his little stove when winter caught him,
and moored to the rocks on the coast of Labrador.
He walked ashore on the ice of the cove each day,
collecting firewood along the rocky shingle,
chopping ice and loading it onto the deck for water,
and worked about the boat in the short, cold light.

In the long, long nights, wind howling at his chimney,
and tiny flakes of snow dusting his face,
he lay many hours, impatient in the darkness.
He listened to the booming of the ice
and wished he had more paraffin for the lamp.

He lay awake one night, and could not tell the time,
but there was brightness at the porthole. He went
    on deck.
The sky was alight with silent, flickering flames.
He stood in a cauldron of snow and frozen trees.
The flames licked up on all sides to the sky.
And this time, in the icy, ringing silence,
he heard men singing in an ancient tongue,
and the sound of distant music,
as if just on the far side of a hill.

Spring found him beating south to meet her.
But the wind was easterly and full of rain
as he left the sheltering lee of Belle Isle,
and something — he never knew what — turned
    him west,
inside the maritimes of Canada.

He sailed all night, his eyes fixed on the line
between the sky and the silhouette of trees,

his ears ringing with the strain of listening
for the gentle slap of waves on sand or stone
or the chilling whisper of keel in bottom weeds.
When light returned, he found himself
standing up the center of the river,
and the land far-flung on either side.

The swell of the sea was gone; the chilly breeze
in the morning sun was warm and smelled of evergreens.
The river gulls were whiter, daintier than
the gray old ocean dogs
who'd harried him down the coast of Labrador.
The firm, warm wind of the afternoon buried
his leeward rail and left two rows of bubbles
straight as a wild duck's flight
as far as he could see behind him toward the sea.

He passed close to some fishing boats —
he waved, and they waved back,
but he did not know the tongue they spoke —
and came one day at last to Lac St. Pierre.

In the morning he stopped at a farmer's dock
to barter for meat and milk and vegetables,
and thus he met Marie.

The dragon-fires burned bright that night,
the lights danced all across the sky;
he heard the singing from beyond the sky.
But he turned away, toward two eyes
that held him fast as any chain.
He and his boat would never taste salt again.
She lay at the dock, all neatly furled,
and tried to forget about the world
that they would never see.

Their home was on an island in the river.
Fishing and farming were work that Olav knew.
The men of Lac St. Pierre
found Olav a place among them;
for he could row all day and half the night
and never seem to need to stop for rest,
and easily do the work of two.
They swore he ate enough for five.

When Marie felt the child kicking in her,
she knew it was a boy. But she could not know
she bore a dragon in her womb;
that somewhere in the Arctic night
a dragon-spirit had left the shimmering hall
and was marching south across the ice
to meet her in the spring.

He came the night the river ice went out,
and his cries were mingled with the roar
of black ice grinding in the night,
of dark ice grumbling to the sea,
drowning his mother's agony.
Olav Eriksson stood by.
The veins in his arm swelled black when he clenched his
    fist.
He smoothed the wisps of hair
from her sweating forehead and her screaming eyes
and heated hopeless water on the stove.

So great this baby was!
Olav cursed his red-faced race
and kissed his tiny bride.
The baby seemed to fight his own way into life
and flayed her love alive.

She shook her head from side to side
as the flower blooming in her died.
How much she wanted not to die! —
but the room grew dim as her eyes bled dry.

If any man on Lac St. Pierre
could run across the ice to town that night,
his name was Eriksson.

But the river muttered in its winter bed
and rumpled the heaving blankets on its back.
It heard the baby cry and smiled
and grumbled softly to itself.
It waited for the man who had to take its dare,
it let him skip a moment on its back,
then turned and took him in.
Even such a man as he
could live for only minutes in the ice
Before he lost the will to live a wifeless life.

Later that night the ice, as if alive,
reared up and overwhelmed the shore,
rumbled down the banks, scraping them clean,
rolling trees before it, crushing Olav's dock,
and returned Ulf Thorsson's little boat to the sea.

Two days and nights had lingered by
till anyone noticed the boat and dock were gone,
that there were no smoke or lights on Eriksson's Island.
They found them, dead baby sucking a dead breast.
But when they made to cover them, tenderly,
the baby stirred, and seemed to live.
So very feeble was his flame
that it was weeks before he cried,
and when his eyes came open, they were blue.

As blue as northern skies are blue,
with skin as red as lobster claws.
Long-muscled like his father, too,
and hair as soft as kittens' paws.

And that was all the folks that Martin ever had.
He never even saw his mother's grave, or wanted to,
because, the priest said carelessly one day,
his coming at such a time had killed her.
An island farmer's family took the boy,
they named him Martin Gariépy,
and raised him as their own.
They set his little hands to work the sandy soil
brought down by the river and dropped in a hundred
    islands.
His arms grew straight and strong,
and his tongue, so built for nordic phrase,
wrapped itself about the rapid French
the village spoke; but knew not discontent,
until one day, at ten, not knowing why —
he spoke, in later years, of something in the sky:
it seemed to him that something shimmered in the
    sky —
he dropped his hoe and stole a boat.

He landed on the southern shore and walked into the
   woods,
the mining towns, the open-fielded farms, the villages.
He traveled with a sense of the island behind him;
Like his father before him, he kept his native land
between his shoulder blades until it disappeared.
No one noticed him. He crossed a river,
flowing north — the Richelieu — committing himself,
unknowing, to a life west of Champlain.
Somewhere he wandered across an unguarded frontier,
and the only language he knew faded behind him.

He heard a strange new tongue and saw strange men:
great, bearded giants in smelly wool shirts and pants,
leather boots, and rough and laughing voices.
His eyes grew wide with the wonders they saw,
and his little body gaunt as a sparrow's claw.

Three months of summer he floated south
through the roaring, booming north country.
Lumber, marble, pulpwood, hematite, granite.
The stream flowed strongly, and he swept along,
not knowing where he went, or why,
but knowing only that he had to go;

not caring, and picking up, as he went along,
some scraps of food and phrase to feed himself.

Then the stream slowed, and the little dragon-man
was left to circle in a secret pool:
a lonely, tortured land of ancient beech,
tiny clapboard villages, and sugarbush.
Here the great white glaciers' icy pride
had dimmed and rotted, just before they died.
And when their carcasses were gone, devoured
by the carrion sun, they left the country writhing,
as a horse's hoof leaves a snake behind it, writhing.

A land of small, impulsive, gravel hills,
mosquitoes swarming in the valley swamps
and black flies crawling on his neck and arms.
Bloody scratches on his bony wrists.
His belly heaved with sudden fear one day
when his footstep startled a dozing bear,
big and dark as a mountain, in a blackberry patch.

Now and then he came across a road,
and oftentimes a tiny farm.
The clearings always startled him,
and the joy of a pasture was rare:

deep grass and cows
and black crows in yellow grain patches;
sun-warm boulders by meadow pools
where he sat and watched his shadow
shoo the tiny trout from stone to stone,
and marveled at the liquid clouds of smoke
that curled up from the mud
in the silent crystal atmosphere.

One morning he caught a baby cottontail
in the corner of a new stone wall,
too young to know that it should run from him.
He raised a stone to kill it, but let it go.
So he begged for scraps at kitchen doors
and stole his clothes from wild apple trees,
where they were hung on the thorns to dry.
The autumn nights were growing colder now,
The oaks and beeches were beginning to turn
and whispered to each other, rustling,
in the still, expectant, golden afternoons.

He asked for work now whenever he stopped.
But his arms were spindle-thin,
and his knees big burls on maple sapling legs.
There was no sentiment in the hearts

of those who turned him away from their doors.
Sentiment was a thing too dear to nurse
amid the boulders of Tug Hill.

One day a ridge he walked gave way to briers,
and he slid his way through dead leaves down its slope.
There, in a rocky hollow between the hills
by a tiny chuckle of a stream half-choked with alders,
he found a graying farmhouse and a barn
and a straggling, rocky pasture wih bony cows.
There was no baying dog to challenge him,
only the clucking of chickens in the yard
and the squeak of the gate as he crept to the door.

Lottie answered, wiping her hands on her apron.
Though Lottie possessed small sentiment,
the chilly smell of loneliness, like mold
in a dirt-floored cellar, was always in her house.

At thirty, she was married half her life,
yet she bloomed almost as on her wedding day.
There were no children noisy in her home,
and Martin's arms were very thin.
Her man had never known a god,
and she saw the bony little vagabond

cross himself with crowfoot hands before he ate.
So she tooted Luther in from work
and showed him her new child.

She stole from Luther's whiskey poke
to make him clothes, took her beating,
and stole some more for books.
She sat him by the stove on winter nights,
made him trudge across the pages of McGuffey
and fumble through the muddle of his numbers.
She weaned him from a faith he'd never known
and told him stories from her simple, narrow book.
Now and again her voice would fill with tears,
and Martin came to share her hate
of the smell of the poison killing her man.

As one man died, another was born.
The fields were strewn with forsaken booty
of retreating glaciers. Martin carried each stone
in his skinny arms, staggering, and built
great monuments of rock in every field.
His young back wrenched and twisted
when boulders turned his plowshare up.
The bullied horses would not stop for him.
He had to drag the row, dig in at the end,
and begin it all over again.

His eyes grew squinted from the sun
and faded blue as faded shirts are blue.

Sometimes at night — dew falling silently;
creek-chuckling night, alive with crickets —
he started awake in his bed beneath the rafters,
and heard a distant cry that made no sound,
and knew somehow the lights were in the sky,
flickering and flaming in the northern sky.

He lay in the brief dark of the summer night
and strained his ears to hear the cry again.
The smells of the house filled the air around him --
of kerosene, smoked hams, and ashes in the stove.
But through the window open to the north,
a breath of colder air stirred the curtain,
and he caught the smell of an arctic wind
blowing off the ice.
Breakfast found him silent, and his eyes
ten thousand miles away.

In winter they felled great hardwood trees
and drew the logs to the loading yard.
Each year Martin's end of the crosscut saw
pulled faster and bit deeper, and Luther's less,
until one day, without his usual warning,

old Luther dropped his handle and stood up straight,
clutching at his shirt. A moment later
he fell into the sawdust on the snow and died.

So Martin grew to be a man: six feet of Norway
with a lobster's skin and a pale blue northern eye.
He made the strangled pastures bloom with life
and watched the bones melt from his cattle's sides.
One Saturday in Camden, at the feed store,
to win a bet, he slung a harness on his back
and walked four bags of grain two times around the green.
His trade was sharp, his softness hard as boulders,
but anyone who needed help could find his farm.

In church he sat with Lottie in their pew,
and did not seem to see the eager eyes
that sought his from beneath the rims of bonnets.
Nor did he notice Lottie every day,
watching him work from the kitchen door.
Until at breakfast one late winter morning
he looked up from his oats and met her eyes,
and blushed. Oatmeal for their wedding breakfast,
and for their honeymoon, they hurried home to milking.

Their happiness was the smell of spring.
It was as if their lives had wintered since their birth.

The snow shrank grumbling back into the woods.
The new hay greened among the stubble.
A woodchuck tumbled from his pile of rocks
and felt the strengthening sun upon his fur.

In the creek bottom the pussy willows burst,
and the trout fought their way from the pastures
to the summer coolness of the woods above.
And Lottie knew something she had never known:
the first faint ecstasy of life within her.

They drove one steaming summer day
to Lester Graves's farm to raise a house.
The folks from all around were there.
They needed Martin's back beneath the beams,
his quiet voice, his easy competence.
They wanted Lottie's salt pork and beans
and her bubbling laugh beside the iron stove.
The stove was set up in the grassy yard,
to go into the house before the doors were framed.

The frame was up by noon, and the rafters
up and pegged in place by four o'clock.
The women set the pot and platters out,
the pastor said grace, and everyone fell to.

There came a muffled grumbling from the west,
a faint, but deep vibration from the ground,
and everyone looked up from the table to see
a boiling of black clouds above the hills,
a thunderstorm rolling off Ontario.
It's Henry Hudson's men, the pastor cried,
playing at tenpins in the glen. They laughed.
But Martin didn't laugh. He shook his head at Lottie.
It had felt to him, he said, as if some god
had beat upon the earth with a mighty hammer.

They picked up the wooden benches and the board,
food and all, and carried them into the barn.
Nothing at all; the storm would pass;
bad for the milk tonight, but good for the grass.

Martin and Lester and Norman Graves
had just returned to the great black stove
to salvage four last pots of early corn.
The iron top hissed as the first big drops
spattered on the hot black plates
and danced about until they vaporized.

But then they felt a sudden copper tension,
a humming green expectation in the air.
A moment more, and the world exploded in fire.

For long moments afterward no one could breathe.
Inside the barn, the table lay upon the floor
with the women and all the scattered food.
When finally someone raised his head to look,
the sugar maple beside the stove was split,
and the range lay in a smoking, hissing heap.
The three men lay in the grass around it, still.
Norman's head had been cloven like a walnut;
he poured a bright and quiet red molasses
onto the steaming yellow ears of corn.
Lester and Martin were jackstrawed in the grass.
Lester was dead. Somehow, Martin was not.

He lay in the front bedroom many days
and slept and slept and did not move.
Lottie was there the whole time,
so she was there when he opened his eyes.
The blue eyes fixed upon her own.
They flickered, and they grinned.
She tasted her own warm tears.
But then her stomach twisted as he smiled,
and she found herself retching
into the sink by the kitchen pump.
For spittle crept from the corners of his mouth;
his eyes the shallow puddles of an imbecile.

He could not be made to feel sufficient grief
when one day he was somehow made to understand
that Lottie had lost the baby.

I sit here leaning against a maple stump
and watch him cross the pasture in the sun.
It looks as though some farmer's scarecrow,
disgusted with the wind and rain and castoff shirts,
has run off his job and, wandering through the fields,
has come to share my sandwiches and beer.
A pair of filthy, greasy overalls —
I can smell them in my mind already,
above the gunpowder scent of the fresh-cut stone —
hangs on the knotty back that still can swing
four hundred pounds, but is no longer proud.
His trouser cuffs are torn clear to his knees
and flap about his ankles as he walks.

He stumbles gaily, not realizing why:
both eyes no longer focus on the ground.
The thin tobacco juice runs slowly down
the crevices in his chin and drips to his chest.
Now and again he raises a dirty hand
and wipes it off as if he stroked a beard.
Lottie has made him a canvas bib to wear.

But he's been using it to blow his nose.
His halloo is pleasant and conventional,
recalled perhaps from other afternoons
or rehearsed by Lottie as he left the house.

He's come to help me load the stone, he says,
but seems confused about it — something I said
last time, two days ago — something about
being careful not to mar the faces
of the blocks. What was it that you said?

His eyes, as I explain, stare at me, through me, past me,
as if my voice were coming from behind
my right shoulder. They see nothing. They look
for all the world like empty Wedgwood plates.

I want to reach and take them in my hands.
I want to shake them till they cry they see! —
they see them! the lights in the northern sky!
until they dream of dragons once again.

www.bunkerhillpublishing.com
First published in 2011
by Bunker Hill Publishing Inc.
285 River Road, Piermont
New Hampshire 03779, USA

10 9 8 7 6 5 4 3 2 1

Library of Congress Control Number: 2010942804

ISBN 10: 1-59373-089-6

ISBN 13: 978-1-59373-089-5

Published in the United States by Bunker Hill Publishing

Designed by Peter Holm, Sterling Hill Productions

Printed in Canada